@RosenTeenTalk

DEATH

Kathleen A. Klatte

ROSEN
PUBLISHING

NEW YORK

Published in 2021 by The Rosen Publishing Group, Inc.
29 East 21st Street, New York, NY 10010

First Edition

Editor: Elizabeth Krajnik
Designer: Michael Flynn
Interior Layout: Rachel Rising

Photo Credits: Cover, pp. 3, 5 fizkes/Shutterstock.com; cover, pp. 1, 6, 8, 10, 12, 14, 18, 20, 22, 24, 28, 30, 32, 34, 38, 40, 42 Vitya_M/Shutterstock.com; cover Cosmic_Design/Shutterstock.com; cover Denis Gorelkin/Shuttestock.com; pp. 3, 17, 21, 24 RichLegg/E+/Getty Images; pp. 3, 27 Drew Horne/Shutterstock.com; pp. 3, 37 hxdbzxy/Shutterstock.com; pp. 3, 45 Pamela Au/Shutterstock.com; p. 6 Photographee.eu/Shutterstock.com; p. 7 Orawan Pattarawimonchai/Shutterstock.com; p. 9 StunningArt/Shutterstock.com; p. 10 Angel_AMX/Shutterstock.com; p. 10 pil76/Shutterstock.com; p. 11 pixelheadphoto digitalskillet/Shutterstock.com p. 12 sfam_photo/Shutterstock.com; p. 13 Marta Design/Shutterstock.com; p. 14 Terry Vine/The Image Bank/Getty Images; p. 15 Erin Deleon/Shutterstock.com; p. 18 Dave Newman/Shutterstock.com; p. 19 pathdoc/Shutterstock.com; p. 20 Urilux/E+/Getty Images; p. 23 Syda Productions/Shutterstock.com; p. 25 Kzenon/Shutterstock.com; p. 28 Image Source RF/Steve Prezant/Image Source/Getty Images; p. 29 Jeff Greenough/Getty Images; p. 31 Prostock-studio/Shutterstock.com; p. 32 RapidEye/E+/Getty Images; p. 33 NKM999/Shutterstock.com; p. 34 Sabphoto/Shutterstock.com; p. 35 marekuliasz/Shutterstock.com; p. 38 Russell Underwood/Getty Images; pp. 39, 43 Daisy Daisy/Shutterstock.com; p. 40 Paddy Photography/ Moment/Getty Images; p. 41 Rawpixel.com/Shutterstock.com; p. 42 Borysevych.com/Shutterstock.com; p. 43 Daisy Daisy/Shutterstock.com.

Some of the images in this book illustrate individuals who are models. The depictions do not imply actual situations or events.

Cataloging-in-Publication Data

Names: Klatte, Kathleen A.
Title: Death / Kathleen A. Klatte.
Description: New York : Rosen Publishing, 2021. | Series: Rosen teen talk
Identifiers: ISBN 9781499468069 (pbk.) | ISBN 9781499468076 (library bound)
Subjects: LCSH: Death--Juvenile literature. | Funeral rites and ceremonies--Juvenile literature. | Grief--Juvenile literature.
Classification: LCC GT3150.K58 2021 | DDC 393--dc23

Manufactured in the United States of America

CPSIA Compliance Information: Batch #BSR20. For further information contact Rosen Publishing, New York, New York at 1-800-237-9932.

Find us on

CONTENTS

Chapter 1

Suddenly Gone

My aunt Pat died this morning. A neighbor came and told us. He'd gone to her store to get rolls for breakfast and there was a sign on the door saying the ambulance had taken Aunt Pat to the hospital.

Dad made some phone calls. No one had had a chance to call us yet because it happened so suddenly. They think Aunt Pat had a heart attack.

I don't understand how this happened. I just saw Aunt Pat a couple days ago. She wasn't sick, and she wasn't that old. She was the same age as my mom.

The funeral will be on Friday. Mom let me pick t flowers we're sending to the funeral home. I chose ligh purple because that was Aunt Pat's favorite color.

Mom is especially sad. She's been crying a lot the past few days. She and Aunt Pat were best friends. The funeral is going to be hard on all of us.

WHY DO PEOPLE DIE?

People die for lots of reasons. Some people die from natural causes. It's not a shock when someone who's old or very sick dies. It's mostly just sad.

It's hard when someone you love is sick or in pain. Some people find comfort when those who've been sick for a long time die. It means they aren't suffering anymore.

Sometimes people die suddenly. That can be scary. People die in **accidents** or because of crime. The news sometimes talks about soldiers who've died during a war. This can be very upsetting.

Another word you might have heard is suicide. That's when someone kills themselves because they don't want to keep living. Suicide is hard for many people to understand.

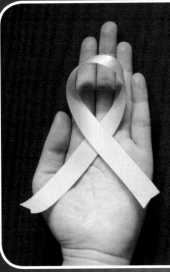

SUICIDE PREVENTION

Asking for Help

Suicide is one of the leading causes of death for young people. Sometimes life can seem too hard and people don't know where to go for help. The National Suicide Prevention Lifeline is a group that can help people who are thinking of ending their own life. Their website is

https://suicidepreventionlifeline.org/

SO MANY FEELINGS

There's no right or wrong way to feel when you hear that someone has died. Different people feel different things, and that's OK!

You might not feel sad at first. It can be shocking if someone suddenly dies. It's scary if there's a big accident on the highway or a fire nearby.

You might feel anger toward a careless driver or even at doctors who couldn't save someone's life. You might even feel relief if someone has been sick or in pain for a long time. All these feelings make sense.

If you feel angry, it's important to work through your anger in a safe way. Going for a run or throwing a ball might help. Just be sure you're in a safe place and that a trusted adult knows where you are.

DEATH IN THE MEDIA

Turning on the news can be upsetting. There always seem to be stories about war, **terrorism**, or accidents that kill people. Sometimes these things happen very far away. That's not always so scary.

Other bad things can happen very close to where you live. You may hear about a school shooting or a dangerous storm. It's normal to worry when that happens. If something bad happens nearby, your school may bring in **counselors** to help you.

LIVE
NEWS
4:35 20

LIVE

BREAKING

NEWS

BREAKING NEWS

FAST AND FIRST

SHERIFF: SUSPECT IN SCHOOL SHOOTING IN CUSTODY
SCHOOL BRINGING IN COUNSELOR FOR STUDENTS

It's OK to be upset when you see a news story about people who've died. Those things actually happened to someone. If you're really worried, you should talk to a trusted adult.

WHAT HAPPENS WHEN SOMEONE DIES?

When someone dies, a doctor fills out a special report. It's called a death certificate. It lists the reason the person died and when it happened. A death certificate is an important **legal** paper.

If someone dies of old age or illness, they've died of natural causes. Most times, pathologists don't perform autopsies on people who've died of natural causes.

If there are questions about the way someone died, an autopsy may be needed. This is when a special kind of doctor called a pathologist studies the person's body to figure out exactly how they died. An autopsy is always performed if police think a crime might have been committed.

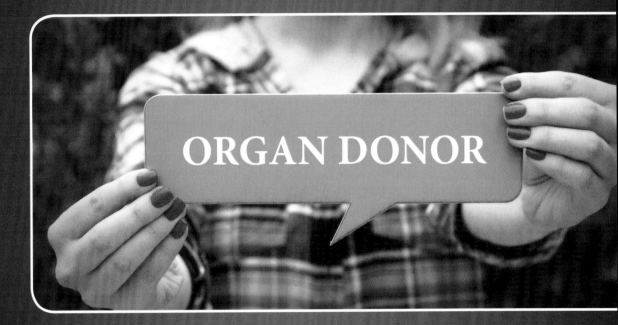

DONATE!

Some people carry a card in their wallet that says they're an organ donor. An organ donor is someone who says it's OK for doctors to take out parts of their body after they've died to give them to people who need them. There are many sick people on organ **transplant** waiting lists. You can learn more about organ donation at **https://www.organdonor.gov/**

WHAT HAPPENS TO THEIR BODY?

People have different beliefs about what happens to a person when they die. No matter the belief, it's important to remember that everything that made them a person is gone now. Their body is just flesh and bone.

Sometimes someone's body is very badly damaged when they die. No one wants to remember their loved one that way. Instead of viewing the body, a nice photograph is displayed. This is called a closed-**casket** funeral.

Autopsies don't hurt the person in any way. Nothing that's done as part of the funeral hurts them either. Some **religions** say embalming and autopsies shouldn't be performed. They say that the body shouldn't be changed in any way after death.

EMBALMING

Embalming is a way of **preserving** a body after death. This is done if the body needs to be sent somewhere. It's also done if the body is going to be viewed as part of the funeral.

Chapter 2

A Blessing?

On Sunday morning, we read in the newspaper that my friend's younger brother was hit by a car. I was very mad at the driver at first. Then we found out that Timmy had run into the road without looking. It wasn't the driver's fault at all.

Tonight, at church, the pastor announced that Timmy had died. Everyone says it's a blessing because his brain was hurt so badly. He never woke up after the accident.

I don't see how it's a blessing for a little kid to die. No parents should have to bury their child. I'm really worried about my friend. He and his brother were super close. I'm going to call and talk to him. I hope he's OK.

My family went to Timmy's funeral. It was very hard to see Timmy's family so upset. I wish they weren't going through this.

WHAT DOES IT MEAN?

It's common for people to feel uncomfortable talking about death. They tend to use a lot of sayings. Some of them sound very formal. It can be confusing. You know the person is trying to be kind, but you're not really sure what the sayings mean.

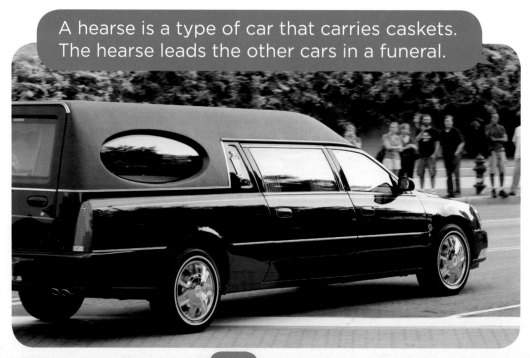

A hearse is a type of car that carries caskets. The hearse leads the other cars in a funeral.

Many words about death may be unfamiliar to you. An obituary is a written article about the dead person's life. A eulogy is a speech about them.

COMMON PHRASES

WHAT THEY SAID	WHAT THEY MEANT
"He passed away."	He died.
"They're in **mourning**."	They're sad because someone they love has died.
"She's in a better place now."	She's not sick or in pain anymore.
"My condolences for your loss."	I'm very sorry that someone close to you died.
"He was laid to rest."	His body was buried.

FUNERAL ARRANGEMENTS

A phrase you might hear is "funeral arrangements." This means the plans for what happens to the body of the person who's died. These plans are usually made by the person's family. Sometimes people leave their own instructions for what they want done when they die.

Funerals are usually held about three days after someone dies. Some religions say a person should be buried no more than one day after they have died.

Very often, this is based on a person's religious beliefs. It generally includes a gathering of the person's friends and family. Sometimes this includes a request for people to make donations to a charity in the dead person's name.

LIFE INSURANCE

A life insurance policy protects the family of someone who has died. A person pays a fee to an insurance company every month. When they die, money is paid to their family. This money can help make sure a family can stay in their home or continue running their business.

WHAT'S A FUNERAL HOME?

A funeral home is a place people go to make arrangements for someone who's died. A person called a funeral director helps the family pick out a casket. They also arrange flowers and photographs of the person in the funeral home.

Sometimes people have a wake. This is generally held at a funeral home. It's a time when people gather quietly to remember the person who's died. Usually, people can see the person's body in the casket. It's not scary. They're dressed nicely and just look like they're asleep.

Sometimes people choose cremation. This is when the dead person's body is placed in a machine that burns the body to ashes. Cremation doesn't hurt the person because they're already dead.

WHAT HAPPENS AT A FUNERAL?

A funeral is a **ceremony** to remember someone who's died. Sometimes it's a religious service. It can also be a gathering of friends and family to share memories.

At some funerals, each person lays a flower on the casket. At others, the casket might be lowered into the grave. People then place a handful of dirt into the grave.

Be Respectful

If you go to a funeral or wake, you should dress neatly. Be quiet and respectful of others. If you're comfortable with it, you can share your memories of the person.

Taking the dead person's body to its final resting place is part of most funerals. This means taking their casket or cremated remains to be buried.

Funerals take place as a way for people to say goodbye to their loved ones and remember their lives. Different religions and **cultures** have different kinds of funerals.

Fact!

A columbarium is a special building that holds urns. An urn holds the ashes of people who've been cremated. The urns are set into small spaces called niches.

Chapter 3

A Terrible Accident

A boy I used to know died in a car accident. A lot of people said that since he was a teenager, he must have been drunk or on drugs. This made his friends and family really mad.

John was a good guy. He had just graduated from high school. He got a construction job for the summer and played guitar in a band at night. The police think he might have swerved to avoid hitting a deer. It was just a terrible accident.

The doctors tried very hard, but they couldn't save his life. The casket was closed at John's funeral because the doctors had to shave off his hair. His mom knew he wouldn't like that. Instead, she put a picture of John with his guitar on his casket.

John's injuries were so bad that he had to be taken to the hospital in a helicopter. The doctors tried their hardest to save him. It's not their fault he died.

WHAT'S A CEMETERY?

A cemetery is a place where dead people are buried. Cemeteries are very quiet and peaceful. Each grave is marked with who's buried there. Some grave markers are made of metal and others are made of stone. They usually say the person's name, their date of birth, and their date of death.

It's important to be quiet and respectful when you visit a cemetery. Other visitors are thinking about their loved one. A funeral may be taking place.

People visit cemeteries to remember people who have died. Some people like to say things while they're visiting the person's grave. Others like to keep quiet and think.

MILITARY FUNERALS

Members of the military who are killed in action and **veterans** often have very **elaborate** funerals. Someone from the person's branch of the military helps the family make arrangements. Military funerals usually include a gun **salute**. A person plays a song called "Taps" on a **bugle**.

DIFFERENT PEOPLE HAVE DIFFERENT FEELINGS

People don't always feel the same way when someone dies. Your mom or dad might be very sad that an older **relative** died. They may have good memories of spending time together. You might just know them as a name on a holiday card or someone you visited every few years.

You might be much more upset at the death of your family pet. You might also have felt very sad when your favorite basketball player died. There's no right or wrong way to feel.

It's important to respect how other people feel. You might not feel the same way, but you should always be kind to people who are grieving.

LOSING A PARENT

Losing a parent is really hard. It's sad to lose one of the people who's taken care of you your whole life. You might also be worried about a lot of important things.

You may wonder if you need to move or if someone else will take care of you now. It's very important to talk to your family. They need to know what's on your mind. If you're old enough to ask a question, you're old enough to receive an answer.

A psalm is one of the hymns from the Old Testament book of Psalms. People often read Psalm 23 during Christian and Jewish funerals. Many people find its words comforting.

Helping Make Arrangements

If you feel up to it, you can ask to help make arrangements for your parent's funeral. You might help choose the flowers. You could also make a copy of your favorite photo to be buried with them.

SPEAKING AT THE FUNERAL

You may be asked if you'd like to speak at your parent's funeral. You might read a prayer or a poem that's meaningful to you. You might tell people your favorite memory of your parent. If you don't feel comfortable speaking, that's OK too.

IT HURTS SO MUCH!

Grief is an **extreme** form of sorrow that people feel when someone they love dies. It can involve lots of other feelings too. Sometimes grief can affect the way your body feels. You might feel tired all the time or almost as if you're coming down with the flu.

Sometimes the universe has terrible timing. The last time you saw the person who died might not have been so good. Perhaps you were rude or had an argument. It's important to remember that this had nothing to do with them dying. It's not your fault.

It takes time to understand all the things you feel when someone dies. Dr. Elisabeth Kübler-Ross made a list of the stages of grief. Not everyone goes through all of them, but many people do.

THE FIVE STAGES OF GRIEF

DENIAL	You just can't believe that the person has died.
ANGER	You're mad that they left you.
BARGAINING	You try to make a deal with God or the universe to give back the person who died.
DEPRESSION	You're extremely sad that the person died.
ACCEPTANCE	You get used to the idea that they're dead.

Chapter 4

I Miss Grandma

Yesterday was awful. I was supposed to have skating practice after school, but a machine broke at the rink. The ice melted, so I had to go to the hospital with my mom instead.

My grandma was in the hospital because of her heart. I only got to see her once, a couple of days ago. The hospital let kids visit the **ICU** for Easter.

Grandma was going to come and live with us when she got better. But yesterday she got sicker. She died last night. I know she was tired and missed Grandpa, but I really wanted her to come and live with us. I already miss her a lot.

Many young people share the experience of having a grandparent who has died. You can reach out to your friends and ask them what they do when they miss their grandparent.

FORMAL MOURNING

A long time ago, there used to be many rules about how to act when someone died. People were supposed to dress a certain way. They weren't supposed to do anything fun for a long time.

This seems very fussy and old-fashioned to us now, but it was useful. Everyone recognized the signs of mourning. If there was black cloth on the front door, no one would bother the family. If someone wore a black veil or armband, other people knew that they might be easily upset.

Acts of Kindness

Being kind and helpful to the family of someone who's died is a good practice. You can offer to walk their dog or put out their trash bins.

It's a common practice to bring food when someone has died. Cooking a meal is one less thing for the family to have to think about.

MOURNING COLORS

In many Western cultures, black is the color of mourning. In other cultures, people wear white. In other parts of the world, purple, yellow, or red might be worn.

REMEMBERING SOMEONE WHO'S DIED

You can do a lot of things to remember someone who's died. Many people like to visit a loved one's grave. They might plant flowers in spring or lay a wreath for the holidays.

Some religions do special things, such as lighting candles, on the anniversary of a person's death.

Other people prefer to do something more active. Perhaps your loved one had a favorite **charity**. You might be able to **volunteer** in their name.

It can also be nice to make something to help you remember the person who died. It could be a scrapbook of favorite photos or a box of mementos.

Last Will and Testament

A will, or testment, is a legal document. It says who a person's belongings should go to when they die. Usually a will lists things like a house or car. Sometimes a person leaves instructions for money to be given to someone in the future to pay for college or their wedding. It might also say who should receive family **heirlooms**.

GETTING BACK TO NORMAL

Losing someone you love is very hard to handle. Getting back to your normal **routine** can be hard too. It can hurt to see an empty seat at the table or your loved one's things around the house.

It can also hurt the first time you go out after a funeral. Everything may seem too loud and too close. You might think that people are being mean. They probably don't mean to be. They just don't know what's going on in your life.

Some people plan ahead. They have a lawyer write instructions in case they become sick, injured, or die.

Chapter 5

Missing Aunt Pat

Aunt Pat died on Labor Day. The first Christmas without her was sad. We always went out to lunch together for the holidays. I'd been making a present for her, but I didn't get a chance to give it to her before she died. I brought the present I'd been making to her grave and left it there for her.

Now my mom and I plan to go out for lunch around the holidays to remember Aunt Pat. We will order her favorite foods and share our fondest memories of her. Then we will go to her grave to decorate it for the holidays.

Aunt Pat was very religious. She believed in heaven. I feel less sad when I imagine that she's in heaven now. I'd be lying if I said I didn't wish she were still alive. I'll always miss Aunt Pat.

Each year at Christmastime, we bring a wreath to Aunt Pat's grave. We talk to her about what's going on in our lives. We tell her we miss her.

GLOSSARY

accident: A sudden event (such as a crash) that isn't planned or intended and that causes damage or injury.

bugle: An instrument like a simple trumpet used mainly for giving military signals.

casket: A box in which a dead person is buried. Also called a coffin.

ceremony: A formal act or event that is part of a social or religious occasion.

charity: An organization that helps people or animals in need.

counselor: A person who provides advice as a job.

culture: The beliefs and ways of life of a certain group of people.

elaborate: Made or done with great care or with much detail. Having many parts that are carefully arranged or planned.

extreme: Very great in degree.

heirloom: A valuable object that's owned by a family for many years and passed from one generation to another.

ICU: Intensive care unit. A section of a hospital where patients who are seriously injured or ill receive care.

legal: Of or relating to the law.

mourning: Great sadness felt because someone has died.

preserve: To prevent a person's body from decaying.

relative: A member of one's family.

religion: An organized system of beliefs, ceremonies, and rules used to worship a god or a group of gods.

routine: A regular way of doing things in a particular order.

salute: To give a sign of respect to a military officer, flag, etc., often by moving your right hand to your forehead.

terrorism: The use of violent acts to frighten the people in an area as a way of trying to achieve a political goal.

transplant: A medical operation in which an organ or other part that has been removed from the body of one person is put into the body of another person.

veteran: A person who has served in the military.

volunteer: To do something to help because you want to do it.

INDEX